Przewalski's Horses

The Child's World®

Published by The Child's World®
1980 Lookout Drive • Mankato, MN 56003-1705
800-599-READ • www.childsworld.com

Acknowledgments
The Child's World®: Mary Berendes, Publishing Director
The Design Lab: Design
Jody Jensen Shaffer: Editing
Red Line Editorial: Photo Research

Photo credits
Anita Huszti/Shutterstock.com: 5, 16; aragami12345s/
Shutterstock.com: 6; Eric Isselee/Shutterstock.com: 22-23;
fotohalo/iStock.com: 12; Jaci Harmsen/Shutterstock.com: 9; Joe
Belanger/Shutterstock.com: rope; kerstiny/Shutterstock.com: 11;
Lizu Zhao/Dreamstime.com: 20; loflo69/Shutterstock.com: 15,
19; rhabdias/iStock.com: cover, 1; Vaclav Volrab/Shutterstock.
com: horseshoes

ISBN 9781626870062
LCCN 2013947298

Printed in the United States of America
Mankato, MN
May, 2014
PA02230

ABOUT THE AUTHOR

Pamela Dell is the author of more than fifty books for young people. She likes writing about four-legged animals as well as insects, birds, famous people, and interesting times in history. She has published both fiction and nonfiction books and has also created several interactive computer games for kids. Pamela divides her time between Los Angeles, where the weather is mostly warm and sunny all year, and Chicago, where she loves how wildly the seasons change every few months.

CONTENTS

The Last Wild Horses

Thousands of years ago, wild horses lived all over Europe and Asia. People started catching and keeping some of the horses. They started raising them for meat. They taught them to pull plows and carry riders. Over time, almost all the wild horses died out. Only one kind still lives today—the Przewalski's (zhuh-VAHL-skeez) horse.

Przewalski's horses lived in Mongolia. Mongolia is a country in Asia. The horses lived on Mongolia's grassy **steppes**. Winters on the steppes were long and cold. Food and water were sometimes hard to find. But these horses were **hardy**. They were able to stay alive.

For a long time, few people lived in Mongolia. The wild horses had plenty of room. But over time, more people came to Mongolia. Przewalski's horses came close to dying out—but they did not.

Some other kinds of horses still live in the wild. But these "wild" horses came from pets that got loose. Przewalski's horses were never anyone's pets.

This Przewalski's horse is enjoying a foggy field in Hungary.

What Do Przewalski's Horses Look Like?

Przewalski's horses are not the most beautiful horses in the world. But they have a special look all their own. They look sort of like tan zebras with almost no stripes. They have tan or reddish brown bodies. Their **muzzles** and bellies are white or cream. A dark stripe runs down the middle of their backs. They have more stripes on the backs of their legs.

In Mongolia, Przewalski's horses are called *takhi*. A single one is called a *takh*. "Takhi" means "spirit" in the Mongolian language.

Most horses have long manes. But Przewalski's horses lose their manes every summer. The manes never get long.

The neck of a Przewalski's horse is short and thick. Its head is large. Its mane is short and brushy. The mane sticks straight up, like a zebra's mane. Both the mane and the tail are dark.

Przewalski's horses' legs get darker toward their hooves.

In the fall, Przewalski's horses grow a longer, heavier coat. The coat keeps them warm during the winter. They even grow beards on their cheeks and throat. In the summer, they lose their heavy coat.

These horses are small and sturdy. A horse's height is measured at its **withers**. Przewalski's horses are only 48 to 56 inches (122 to 142 centimeters) tall. People also say how tall horses are in hands. A hand is 4 inches (10 centimeters). Przewalski's horses stand only 12 to 14 hands high. They are heavily built, though. Sometimes they weigh more than 700 pounds (318 kilograms).

The dark stripe on a Przewalski's horse's back has a name. It is called an "eel stripe."

You can see how this Przewalski's horse's mane stands straight up.

Newborn Przewalski's Horses

In the wild, Przewalski's horses live in herds. The **mares** have babies in the spring or summer. The herd's leader is a **stallion**. He is the babies' father. The adults take good care of their **foals**.

The foals stay with their mothers for 8 to 13 months. At first, they drink only their mothers' milk. Soon they learn to eat plant foods. They play with the other foals. They learn how to stay alive. They stay with the group until they are fully grown. Then it is time for them to leave. They must find new groups of their own.

Wolves sometimes try to attack foals. Mares circle around the foals to keep them safe. The herd's stallion charges at the wolves.

This Przewalski's horse foal was born in a zoo.

Przewalski's Horses in History

People in Mongolia knew about their country's wild horses. But people in the rest of the world did not. They thought wild horses everywhere had died out.

In the late 1800s, Russia was ruled by a czar (ZAR). The czar wanted to know more about lands in Asia. Few outsiders traveled to Mongolia. The czar sent people to learn about the area. One of them was Nikolai Przewalski. Przewalski made trips to Mongolia in the 1870s and 1880s. On his second trip, someone gave him a horsehide and skull. They were from a wild horse! On his third trip, Przewalski saw wild horses himself.

Animals are often named after the people who found them. Wild horses already had a name in Mongolia. But people elsewhere named them after Nikolai Przewalski.

Wild Przewalski's horses were very hard to catch. The herds would run before anyone could get close enough.

You can see this Przewalski's horse has started to grow his autumn beard.

Other outsiders had seen the wild horses earlier. In 1427, a rich German traveled in the Far East. He wrote about some wild horses there. A Scottish doctor saw some in about 1719. But it was Nikolai Przewalski who got people interested.

And they got very interested! Other Europeans and Americans wanted to see the wild horses. Some people wanted to own some. People caught the wild foals. They took them to Europe and the U.S. The trip was slow—sometimes several months. Few of the foals lived through the trip.

By the middle 1900s, American and European zoos had Przewalski's horses. But few horses were left in Mongolia. In the 1960s, only a few wild horses could be found. The last one was seen in 1969. Mongolia's wild horses were gone.

That might have been the end of the story. Luckily, it was not. Some people hoped to bring Przewalski's horses back to the wild. And they worked hard to make that happen.

This Przewalski's horse would have been hard for a European or American to catch.

What Are Przewalski's Horses Like?

Wild Przewalski's horses have never wanted to be around people! They have always run as soon as they saw them. But most of today's Przewalski's horses live in zoos. They are used to having people around. Even so, they do not like to be handled. People have to be careful with them.

These horses like to spend time with each other, though. They like to **groom** themselves and each other. They lick and nuzzle each other. This keeps their coats clean. It is also a way of being friendly.

> You cannot put a saddle on a Przewalski's horse! They do not like to be ridden. And they do not make good pets.

These horses are scratching each other by rubbing together.

How Do Przewalski's Horses Live?

A herd of wild Przewalski's horses has one stallion, several mares, and their foals. Sometimes other stallions form herds of their own. In the wild, each herd moves around within a home range. The home range has food, water, and safe places. The horses eat and drink as they move around. Sometimes they take naps and mud baths, too.

> The steppes of Mongolia have little water. Przewalski's horses can go for days without drinking.

The steppes have wolves and other dangers. Przewalski's horses are always on the lookout for trouble. They can see, smell, and hear very well. At night, one animal stays awake to keep watch.

> Deer and gazelles often stay near herds of Przewalski's horses. That keeps them safer from wolf attacks.

These Przewalski's horses are watching the photographer carefully.

Przewalski's Horses Today

Today, there are Przewalski's horses living in the wild again. In just the last 30 years, people started working to bring the horses back to the wild. It was not easy! First, they brought together a good mix of Przewalski's horses. They got them from different zoos. These horses would have strong, healthy babies.

In 1977, there were only about 300 Przewalski's horses left. Today there are over 1,400.

People set aside some land areas in Mongolia for the horses. These horses had spent their lives in zoos. They needed to get used to living in the wild. First they were turned loose on safe, wide-open land. They learned to get along without people's help. At last, they were ready to be on their own. In the 1990s, the first horses were set free.

Today, about 300 Przewalski's horses live in the wild. They live in Mongolia's Hustai National Park. And they are doing well. Mongolia's wild horses are back where they belong. They are racing across the steppes—just as they did long ago.

This Przewalski's horse lives in a zoo.

Body Parts of a Horse

1. Ears
2. Forehead
3. Forelock
4. Eyes
5. Nostril
6. Muzzle
7. Lips
8. Chin
9. Cheek
10. Neck
11. Shoulder
12. Chest
13. Elbow
14. Forearm
15. Chestnut
16. Knee
17. Cannon
18. Pastern
19. Coronet
20. Hoof
21. Barrel
22. Fetlock
23. Hock
24. Tail
25. Gaskin
26. Stifle
27. Point of hip
28. Croup
29. Loin
30. Back
31. Withers
32. Mane
33. Poll

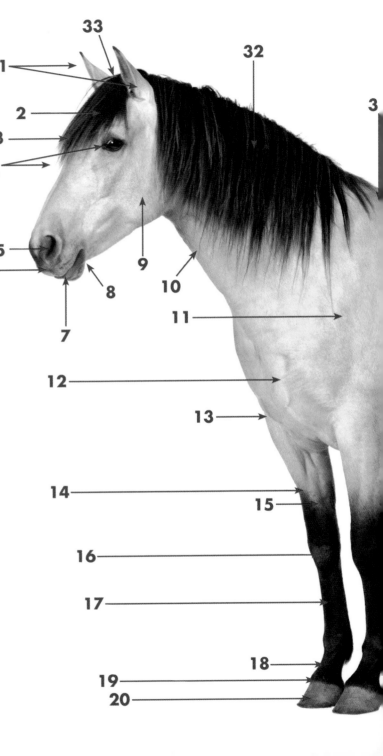

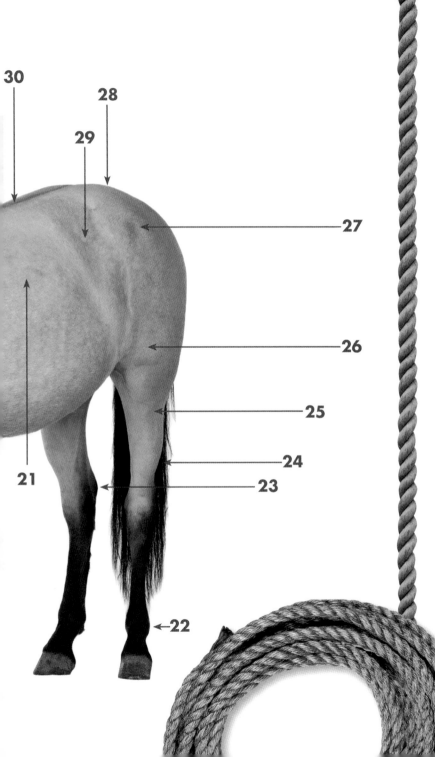

To Find Out More

IN THE LIBRARY

Funston, Sylvia. *The Kids' Horse Book.* Toronto: Maple Leaf Press, 1994.

Ransford, Sandy. *Horses and Ponies.* New York: Kingfisher, 2001.

Swanson, Diane. *Welcome to the World of Wild Horses.* Vancouver: Whitecap Books, 2002.

ON THE WEB

Visit our Web site for lots of links about Przewalski's Horses:

www.childsworld.com/links

Note to Parents, Teachers, and Librarians: We routinely check our Web links to make sure they're safe, active sites—so encourage your readers to check them out!

Glossary

foals (FOHLZ) Foals are baby horses. Adult Przewalski's horses take good care of their foals.

groom (GROOM) To groom an animal is to make it clean and tidy. Przewalski's horses like to groom each other.

hardy (HAR-dee) Hardy means able to stay alive under hard conditions. Przewalski's horses are hardy.

mares (MAYRZ) Mares are female horses. A herd of Przewalski's horses might have several mares.

muzzles (MUZ-zulz) Muzzles are animals' nose and mouth areas. Przewalski's horses have light-colored muzzles.

stallion (STAL-yun) A stallion is a male horse. A Przewalski's horse herd is led by a stallion.

steppes (STEPS) Steppes are dry grasslands. Przewalski's horses live on the steppes of Mongolia.

withers (WIH-thurz) The withers is the highest part of a horse's back. A Przewalski's horse's height is measured at the withers.

Index